P9-CFZ-482

ROBERT PINSKY

Democracy, Culture
and the
Voice of Poetry

PRINCETON UNIVERSITY PRESS

PRINCETON AND OXFORD

Copyright © 2002 by Princeton University Press
Published by Princeton University Press, 41 William Street,
Princeton, New Jersey 08540
In the United Kingdom: Princeton University Press,
3 Market Place, Woodstock, Oxfordshire OX20 1SY

Library of Congress Cataloging-in-Publication Data

Pinsky, Robert.
    Democracy, culture and the voice of poetry / Robert Pinsky.
       p. cm. — (University Center for Human Values)
    Includes index.
    ISBN 0-691-09617-1 (alk. paper)
    1. American poetry—20th century—History and criticism.
    2. United States—Intellectual life—20th century.
    3. Democracy in literatures.   4. Culture in literature.
    5. Poetry.   I. Title.   II. University Center for Human Values
series.

    PS323.5 .P57 2002
    811'.509358—dc21   2002025288

British Library Cataloging-in-Publication Data is available

This book has been composed in Janson

Printed on acid-free paper. ∞

www.pupress.princeton.edu

Printed in the United States of America

1 3 5 7 9 10 8 6 4 2

Contents

vii

To my colleagues and helpers at
The Favorite Poem Project
Boston University
236 Bay State Road

Acknowledgments

I thank the Princeton University Center for Human Values for inviting me to give the Tanner Lectures, and also for providing four vital, insightful and generous public respondents. I am grateful to A. S. Byatt, Jonathan Galassi, John Hollander and Marianna De Marco Torgovnick for their engaged and imaginative discussions of what I said. This published version of the lectures has benefited from their collegiality.

This book approaches its subject partly through the Favorite Poem Project, which has depended upon the vision and support provided by Boston University, the Carnegie Education Foundation, and The National Endowment for the Arts. I am personally grateful to Cliff Becker and William Ivey at the NEA, to Vartan Gregorian at the Carnegie Foundation, and to Jon Westling, president of Boston University, who in addition to his support participated in the Project by reading and memorably discussing Wallace Stevens's poem "The Idea of Order at Key West."

Executive Producer Juanita Anderson, of Legacy Productions, surpassed expectation in producing the video segments. Jeffrey Brown, Jim Lehrer and Les Crystal of "The NewsHour with Jim Lehrer" have helped the segments find their audience.

I am indebted for their help to Christine Bauch, Emily Brandt, Rosemarie Ellis, Maggie Dietz and James Jayo.

Democracy, Culture
and the
Voice of Poetry

I
Culture

The term "culture" with its old agricultural and biological connotations has taken on a new, surprising centrality. In world affairs and in American electoral politics, in geopolitical analysis and in economics, culture has become a kind of ulterior cause of causes. It has been proposed that culture determines the power of a nation to achieve economic development, and that cultural more than political differences underlie electoral contests and atrocities, economic trends and terrorist acts. Cultural clashes seem to have replaced ideological strife. Even the directions and conceptions of science have been seen in cultural terms.

Delivered as a Tanner Lecture on Human Values at Princeton University, April 5–6, 2001. Printed with permission of the Tanner Lectures on Human Values, a Corporation, University of Utah, Salt Lake City, Utah.

1

Far from resisting this trend, I want to consider the voice of poetry—emphasizing its literal or actual "voice"—within the culture of American democracy, amid the tensions of pluralism.

The art of poetry has many of its roots in hierarchical, pre-democratic culture: the flirtations and imperial visions of European courts; the monkish preservations of scholars, the wistful, stylized perception of Asian officials and monks, the folk-narratives, charms and ballads of peasants. Poetry's place in the United States—often presented, I think inaccurately, as no place—presents a node of anxieties about culture itself and about the idea of democracy.

In its long-ago, rather frumpy state, the term "culture"—as in the antiquated phrase "a person of culture"—generated no aura of dread (despite Marxist or Freudian analysis of the mere social fear that one might seem "uncultured"). In its contemporary form, however, the notion of culture evokes anxiety of two contradictory, more or less opposite, kinds.

On one side, there is the nightmare of un-differentiation, a loss of cultural diversity comparable to the loss of biodiversity. Hundreds of languages have died in the last century, with their alphabets and epics and delicate structures. In the terrible closing pages of *Tristes Tropiques*, Claude Levi-Strauss indicates how the mere breath, the very glance, of the observer rapidly destroys differences that evolved for centuries, homogenizing and sterilizing the former abundance. This vision of destruction by an all-consuming dominant culture reminds us of the etymological link between "culture" and the "*colon*": the one who cultivates or scratches the soil, the colonialist.

Closer to home, in the market-generated mass culture that is a successful export, we can see something that resembles the irresistible domination of the colonizers who sweep away and drown out and plow under the ancient range of cultural variety: a kind of internal colonialism, the image of a dominating uniformity that threatens to macerate distinction and level terrain until all are the same.

But the other, obverse dread is of a vicious, tribalized factionalism, the coming apart of civic fabrics through fragmentation, ranging from the tremendous, paranoid brutalities of ethnic cleansing and ruthless terrorism to the petty division of mass culture into niches. Religious difference, racial difference, linguistic difference, even generational difference can seem compounded and hypertrophied by information-age forces. The fanatical concentration on difference and its exploitation by tyranny have been multiplied, accelerated and terribly empowered by modern technology. For example, the speed and reach of contemporary broadcast propaganda have sometimes fit neatly with the activities of killing squads. In this disturbing area, the etymological ghost is culture's relation to "cult," a word denoting arcane forms of worship: the perceived sinister difference of strangers, its ultimate evolution a zeal for extermination.

And here, too, there is a kind of inward, domestic corollary, a dread that goes beyond the breakdown of bowling leagues and civic clubs. In the local microcosm, the cult of xenophobia has its parallels in the paranoid dread of new democratic generations as subliterate media savages. The fear of our own young as letterless, unassimilable barbarians is perhaps an extreme vernacular form of this emotion.

Such are the opposed nightmares of *colon* and cult: fear of suffocation by a centralized overknitting on one side and fear of murderous unraveling from the fringes on the other. These fears—and who can be immune to them?—reflect a profound ambivalence about culture itself, which like the goddess Kali-Parvati both nurtures and destroys. The concept of culture, Stephen Greenblatt has pointed out, "gestures toward what appear to be opposite things: *constraint* and *mobility*"*—

Critical Terms for Literary Study, ed. Frank Lentricchia and Thomas McLaughlin (Chicago: University of Chicago Press, 1995).

normative terms roughly parallel to the unifor-
mities of the colonialist and the fanatacisms of
the cultist. We are simultaneously afraid of constraints making us so much like one another that
we will lose something vital in our human nature, and also in fear of becoming so fluently different, so much divided into alien and brutally
competitive fragments, gangs or fabricated na-
tionalisms, that we cannot survive. In what ways
do these opposed, even contradictory cultural
anxieties share a single source?

For an American poet, the fear of lost differentiation and the fear of excessive differentiation
do indeed embody a single, in fact familiar, anxiety: that of being cut off from memory—forgot-
ten. The shimmering presences of American
mass culture, pervasive and ephemeral, make a
peculiar context for an art associated with memory—with mnemonic rhymes, with the mother
of the Muses, perhaps with epics and sagas.
American memory is so jagged, so polyglot—

often so phantasmagorical—that it has some-times been thought not to exist. A complemen-tary supposition is that American poetry is cut off from American cultural reality.

Unlike memory in a pre-democratic national saga or myth, memory in our high and low cul-tures contains an element of self-negation, a re-lease not into meanings or destinies but into fan-tasy. Gabriel García Márquez has said that the best novel written about Latin America is *The Hamlet*, by William Faulkner. That statement is not only a tribute to the seeds of magic realism in that great novel, but to the quicksilver, reck-lessly fabulous nature of Faulkner's historical imagination. Faulkner's South—or the South of D. W. Griffith or of Toni Morrison—like the West of cowboy movies, the suburbia of classic sitcoms, all have a dreamlike or delirious quality that is conventionally misnamed "mythic."

When Hart Crane concludes his "Proem: To Brooklyn Bridge" with the line "And of the curveship lend a myth to God," he is explicitly writing not a myth but a fantastic invocation of myth itself, a beseeched transformation of "God" and "bridge" and "us lowliest." And the city of Crane or of Ralph Ellison, as much as the city in American gangster movies or screwball comedies, is based not merely on any historical New York or Chicago or San Francisco or Los Angeles, but on the City as a dreamscape of possibilities: a brick and mortar embodiment less of the past than of desire, and more as chorus or antagonist than as a specific, fixed setting. Like the Western town of the movies always about to be tamed, endlessly at the cusp of potential, the City is a civic dream.

But it is historical memory that tempers both of the imagined extremes of culture, the barely habitable polarities of total undifferentiation and total fragmentation. Memory resists uniformity because it registers fine gradations; memory resists the factional because it registers the impure, recombining, fluent nature of culture. It is memory that eventually undermines the apparently total successes of both the colonializing Conquistador and the leveling Visigoth. The fantastic element in democratic memory exaggerates the anxieties of uniformity and fragmentation. Accustomed to practicing an ancient, singular art amid a dazzling mass culture, the American poet is a kind of veteran of these anxieties.

(A theory of American poetry itself could be based on the polarity of cult and *colon*. The fragmentation, ellipsis and implosion of referentiality that have been presented as an experimental or avant-garde style for nearly a hundred years resist the *colon*, the complacent central uniformity. The styles of an often desperate, Anglophile urbanity or an amiable middlebrow accessibility conduct an equally heroic—or at least embattled—resistance to cultural dissolution, a breakdown into provinces and cults.)

The most profound observers of the United

States have seen in our manners, and in the cultural correlatives of our democracy, a version of fragmentation, the dread that we become too unlike one another. Alexis de Tocqueville, in the locus classicus for this viewpoint, associates the separation of individuals into fragments or atoms horizontally, from their peers, with the separation of individuals vertically, from their past and future. Tocqueville writes:

> Thus not only does democracy make every man forget his ancestors, but it hides his descendants and separates his contemporaries from him; it throws him back forever upon himself alone and threatens in the end to confine him entirely within the solitude of his own heart.*

This passage recalls the great classical tag, found in *Gulliver's Travels* as well as in *King Lear*, which notes that the human animal is a puny

Democracy in America, ed. Phillips Bradley (New York: Knopf, 1945), p. 99.

creature: its patchy fur and flimsy hide give inadequate protection; its claws and little teeth are poor weapons. It is a mediocre climber and swimmer, and even its best specimens cannot run as fast as the young or aged of many other species.

This commonplace trope—stripping the human animal of its cultural armature—is traditionally deployed to emphasize certain redeeming human qualities, such as the capacity for reason, free will, or civilization. It is also deployed, as by Lear on the heath, to demonstrate ultimate human frailty and dependence. Tocqueville, in comparing democracy with aristocratic culture, paints the isolation of the single heart in a wilderness that is temporal as well as spatial. To be thrown back "forever" on oneself alone suggests a degree of mobility, a freedom from constraint and dependence, that is potentially exhilarating as well as deranging: a liberation, as well as a void.

That void in its terrible, bleak aspect seems to be in keeping with Tocqueville's most explicit pronouncement about American poetry—a pronouncement that, out of context, as it is usually quoted, can seem comically harsh:

Nothing conceivable is so petty, so insipid, so crowded with paltry interests—in one word, so anti-poetic—as the life of a man in the United States. (*Democracy in America*, p. 74)

But in fact Tocqueville, after observing that the principle of equality "has dried up most of the old springs of poetry," proceeds to ask "what new ones it may disclose." Legends of heroes and gods or angels and demons, old traditions and rituals, all viable material for the poet in aristocratic societies, he says, will not serve poetry in America. He has an interesting notion about the first thing poets in the new world would turn to:

When skepticism had depopulated heaven, and the progress of equality had reduced each individual to smaller and better-known proportions, the poets, not yet aware of what they could substitute for the great themes that were departing together with the aristocracy, turned their eyes to inanimate nature. As they lost sight of gods and heroes, they set themselves to describe streams and mountains. . . . Some have thought that this embellished delineation of all the physical and inanimate objects which cover the earth was the kind of poetry peculiar to democratic ages. But I believe this to be an error, and that it belongs only to a period of transition.

I am persuaded that in the end democracy diverts the imagination from all that is external to man and fixes it on man alone. Democratic nations may amuse themselves for a while with considering the productions of nature, but they are excited in reality only by a survey of themselves. Here, and here alone, the true sources of

poetry among such nations are to be found. . . .
Among a democratic people poetry will not be
fed with legends or the memorials of old traditions. . . . All these resources fail him; but Man
remains, and the poet needs no more. The destinies of mankind, man himself taken aloof from
his country and his age and standing in the presence of Nature and of God, with his passions,
his doubts, his rare prosperities and inconceiv-
able wretchednesses, will become the chief, if
not the sole, theme of poetry among these nations. (*Democracy in America*, pp. 75–76)

And in a rather ringing final paragraph to his
chapter, Tocqueville concludes:

Such are the poems of democracy. The principle of equality does not, then, destroy all the
subjects of poetry: it renders them less numerous, but more vast.

This is a startling declaration by its aristocratic
author. Even if one has no interest whatsoever in

the art of poetry, the movement of the passage's argument should be arresting. Tocqueville's progress from "petty ... insipid ... anti-poetic" to "the destinies of mankind" and materials "less numerous, but more vast" traces an ambitiously prophetic (if perhaps morally ambiguous) trajectory for American culture—pluralistic, omnivorous, syncretic.

I interpret this passage as suggesting not exactly the absence of legends, memorials, heroes, and pantheons but their insufficiency: a worn, jejune quality—a need for something either more candid, or more candidly fantastic. The "old memorials" do not feed the democratic imagination, with its skepticism and isolation. In practice, the inadequacy of "the great themes that were departing together with the aristocracy" has inspired various myth-making projects, including Longfellow's honorable but doomed attempt to make indigenous versions of the "great themes" by way of Paul Revere or Hiawatha. A more enduring invention has been

15

Walt Whitman's extravagant and unrealized idea of the democratic bard—hardly "aloof from his country" but as surely concentrated on the independent human figure, alone with God and Nature, as—equally unmythical, equally rooted in longing—the secularized devotional quatrains of Emily Dickinson.

What Tocqueville's paragraphs say about subject matter in democracy is not merely prophetic of the formal and moral eccentricities of Whitman and Dickinson: her skewed hymns, his breakaway arias. Beyond poetry itself, Tocqueville's idea of democratic nations turning toward a "survey of themselves" raises large questions of constraint and mobility, order and liberty, selfishness and community. Poetry and our ideas about it may offer ways to inspect characteristic dramas of our national life. This Tocqueville passage about poetry and the individual soul adds an historical aspect to certain qualities of poetry that contrast with, perhaps even resist, a

16

mass-scale cultural leveling. Though poetry's history may link it to hierarchical, pre-democratic societies, the bodily nature of poetry links it to the democratic idea of individual dignity. That dual nature of the art gives it a unique significance in the cultural dramas of particularism and universalism, individual and mass.

I don't mean to put popular culture on one side and poetry on another. The drama between human scale and mass scale is embedded to some degree in every modern work. An entire genre of dystopic science-fiction cinema is based on this polarity. The hypnotic mania and unfathomable persistences of minstrel show and sitcom, country music, vaudeville and be-bop reflect that drama, as do similar qualities in our poetry, in the work of poets as different as T. S. Eliot and Allen Ginsberg. The art the poets practice has a special poignance in a society that emphasizes the idea of the individual in the very act of dreaming on an unprecedented mass scale—

17

and so too in a different way do the plaintive, introspective works in "popular idioms" by such artists as Buster Keaton and Charlie Parker. Poetry reflects, perhaps concentrates, the American idea of individualism as it encounters the American experience of the mass—because the art of poetry by its nature operates on a level as profoundly individual as a human voice.

Lyric poetry has been defined by the unity and concentration of a solitary voice—such as might be accompanied by the sound of a lyre, a harp small enough to be held in one hand. It is singular, if not solitary. But the vocality of poetry, involving the mind's energy as it moves toward speech, and toward incantation, also involves the creation of something like—indeed, precisely *like*—a social presence. The solitude of lyric, almost by the nature of human solitude and the human voice, invokes a social presence.

II
Vocality

Dire abandonment, I have read, often makes institutionalized souls, especially children, croon and rock rhythmically: a heartbroken ritual music, a making, a fearsomely minimal created presence. A clinical name for this behavior is autostimulation. The embarrassing hint of masturbation in that term, the grotesque unease or nervous giggle of the association, perhaps reveals an eerie recognition. Just outside the membrane enclosing that wounded isolation, made vivid by contrast, is my ordinary consciousness: engaged yet furtive, communicative yet shamed, teeming with a host of wants and taboos—the word "taboo" embodying the price of our charmed admission to the world of ordinary social stimuli. The regular cadence of the outcast creates a rudimentary other, an illusion of response, that we recognize; the covert sexual fantasies of what we call normal life exemplify a similar principle, the imagination's work of mimesis. The normal soul, too, populates itself with cadences.

The regular, monotonous chant of the abandoned recalls certain vocalizations of our humdrum solitude: say, little repetitious charms of invocation amid the nuisance of some misplaced object—*keys keys keys keys keys*; or the staccato repetition of a one-syllable obscenity, like a muttered ceremony of rage or desperation; or the happier spells of unthwarted celebration, recited at good news or some gratifying experience (*yes yes yes yes yes*); or—perhaps most interesting of all, and closest to the cadenced moans of the devastated—the little half-sung noises we may chant to ease a painful awareness, the pang of embarrassment. My memory of a truly grade-A faux pas can make me half-whisper a syllable like "*dah*" in *prestissimo* monotone to the rhythm of

The Stars and Stripes Forever or *The Mexican Hat Dance*.

These ephemeral protopoems share a rich duality with the auto-stimulation of total distress. The unvarying, solitary rocking or crooning, with its reduction or stylization, perhaps substitutes mimetically for its opposite: a varying, attentive social presence, listening as I lament my lost car keys, curse my mistake, or celebrate the letter announcing good news. The rhythm is like an other, attending to me.

In embarrassment, the tuneless tune I murmur brings back the social world where I brought shame on myself, and imitates the all-too-responsive real presence of others—but in a rudimentary, dwindling simulacrum that distracts me from the awfulness of the actual remembered scene: a tiny cultural creation, attempting to displace or transform memory. And this little mimesis, like the cadenced grunts of loss, has its parallel in poetry.

Nervous muttering resembles a work of art in that it simultaneously sharpens and dislocates a feeling, calling it up but transforming it, maybe blunting it a little by incorporation and mimesis. Insofar as rhythm and repetition accomplish this double action, the little repeated, one-word protopoem differs significantly from anecdote. Anecdote is sociable; perhaps narrative itself is sociable. Life among others in a novel, even a novel entirely in dialogue, is in some essential way *told-about*. The novel overtly tells us what people say and do, immersing us in social reality with an illusion of presentation. In a play, presentation is actual: communal reality, in theatrical performance, exists both as though it were happening and as actually happening.

In a poem, the social realm is invoked with a special intimacy at the barely voluntary level of voice itself. Communal life, whether explicitly included or not, is present implicitly in the cadences and syntax of language: a somatic ghost.

In such a theory, the Industrial-Revolution art form, fiction, reflects the conversation or letters of middle-class people in a town or city: the panicked verbosity of Pamela, the homey enumerations of Robinson Crusoe, the word-wound, shopper-like roaming of Leopold Bloom, all create a social scene from the manufactured web of discourse. The older form of theater is more like a ritual: performance creating actual presences. Maybe that is why theater so often involves the cloying yet somehow apt word "magic." The social world in poetry, according to this paradigm, is neither told about nor presented: it is, precisely, *invoked*: brought into being by the voice. Incantation, rather than the presentation of telling or ritual.

Of course, real works tend to blur or even explode such formulations, defying tidy generic modes of social reality. So too do new forms: film art and opera, both of them influencing and influenced by literature, can give presence a virtually assaultive vividness, as enveloping and fluid as dreams. Technologies like film and broadcast media dismantle any tidy definition of art forms from without, as artists do from within. We routinely recognize qualities in a novel as "poetic" or in a poem as "novelistic" or "dramatic."

Nevertheless, the kinds of art retain attributes, with characteristic terrains—and something deep in poetry operates at the borderland of body and mind, sound and word: double-region of the subtle knot that Donne says makes us man. George Oppen calls up that transitional territory in the fifth section of his poem "Of Being Numerous," with bold contrasts and overlaps among physical fact, cultural artifact, and mind itself:

The great stone
Above the river
In the pylon of the bridge

'1875'

Frozen in the moonlight
In the frozen air over the footpath, consciousness

Which has nothing to gain, which awaits nothing,
Which loves itself.

This passage gains in physicality from the abstract—or at least formal—chiasmic arrange-
ment of vowel-sounds and words in the phrases
"frozen in the moonlight / in the frozen air" and
"nothing to gain, which awaits nothing." Pro-
nouncing such symmetries audibly, or feeling
their virtual sound, quickens our sense of physical breath stirring into social speech: the poetic
quality that poets writing about their art have
associated with a conversation heard through a
door, a drunken song a few streets away, a dis-
tant singer in a foreign tongue. The chiasm of
"nothing to gain ... awaits nothing" is an artifact like the bridge, recognized before it is
interpreted.

Even a dramatic monologue, or a narrated dialogue like Frost's "Home Burial," makes its

voice or voices present to our imagination partly in the half-conscious way I have attributed to poetry: somatically, by invocation, by something akin to the inward reflex of auto-stimulation or the outward wince of embarrassment, a mimesis in rhythmical sound of social life. In Frost's poem, the blank verse becomes more than a vehicle; it is a physical presence: as corporeal as the infant's corpse at the center of the poem's marital argument, and as conventional as the social world that surrounds and infiltrates that same argument. The play of the social and the intuitive is part of the couple's contention, and it is manifest in their voices:

'God, what a woman! And it's come to this,
A man can't speak of his own child that's dead.'

'You can't because you don't know how to speak.
If you had any feelings, you that dug
With your own hand—how could you?—his little
  grave;

26

I saw you from that very window there,
Making the gravel leap and leap in air,
Leap up, like that, like that, and land so lightly
And roll back down the mound beside the hole.
I thought, Who is that man? I didn't know you.
And I crept down the stairs and up the stairs
To look again, and still your spade kept lifting.
Then you came in. I heard your rumbling voice
Out in the kitchen, and I don't know why,
But I went near to see with my own eyes.
You could sit there with the stains on your shoes
Of the fresh earth from your own baby's grave
And talk about your everyday concerns.
You had stood the spade up against the wall
Outside there in the entry, for I saw it.'

'I shall laugh the worst laugh I ever laughed.
I'm cursed. God, if I don't believe I'm cursed.'

This passage of fewer than two hundred words—
barely room for a prose narration to clear its
throat—establishes forcefully the two contend-

ing people with their agonized grief, and within both of the agonists two elements contending for recognition: physical reality on one side, and sensitive decorum or ceremony on the other. Both elements are in the verse. The extreme compression, the more remarkable because the dialogue is credible as speech, is enabled by a physical component, by the artist's arrangements of vocal noises at the threshold of consciousness. The occasional end-rhyme is the least of it: "I saw you from that very window there, / Making the gravel leap and leap in air, / Leap up, like that, like that, and land so lightly / And roll back down the mound beside the hole." Analysis can trace such steps only clumsily and approximately: it is not only the syncopation of repeated words, and not only the vowel in "down the mound" but the contrasting vowel of "hole" that ends the sentence with a rather thudlike rhyme on "roll."

In a way, the most powerful moment in this

conversation is a strange, apparent irrelevance, just before the closing. She has said that "one is alone" and "dies more alone," that "Friends make pretense of following to the grave, / But before one is in it, their minds are turned. . . . " His speech in response culminates in the bizarre line, "Amy! There's someone coming down the road!"

After what she has just said about the underlying frailty, even hypocrisy, of human attachments—"The world's evil"—his sudden, exclamatory concern about a passing neighbor or stranger is grotesque, pathetic, absurd in a way that is quite like life. Embarrassment—a halting consciousness of other people, the sudden barricade of social awareness, obstructing emotion and threatening to take over the mind—is in a way the most basic, irreducible manifestation of social reality. For Frost's characters it is both an obtrusion on their argument and part of its essence. In this unexpected line, bursting from the character as he is about to be left, embarrassment and abandonment—social parallels to the cultural dreads of uniformity and dissolution—conjoin.

III
Self-Consciousness

To some extent, poetry always includes the social realm because poetry's very voice evokes the attentive presence of some other, or its lack: an auditor, significantly absent or present. And in twentieth-century American poetry's incorporation of explicit social material, the tension of social embarrassment and isolation—like the cultural tension of uniformity and dissolution—recurs in our endlessly varying struggles between stereotypes and freedoms, snobberies and realities: an intricate, ineffable process, endlessly banal and aspiring, dire and zany.

The Favorite Poem Project, which became a document (and an example) of that process, began as my response to the peculiar title Poet Laureate Consultant in Poetry to the Library of Congress. The first plan was to make audio recordings of visitors to Washington from around the country, with each person saying the words of a favorite poem and saying something about the poem. In a way by accident, this undertaking filled needs and exerted attractions that led to the remarkable video segments (produced by Juanita Anderson) shown on "The NewsHour with Jim Lehrer"; to the anthology *Americans' Favorite Poems*; and also to thousands of favorite-poem readings, including one at the White House where the readers included then-President Clinton (Emerson's "Concord Hymn") and Hillary Rodham Clinton (Nemerov's "The Makers"), along with District of Columbia schoolchildren and a disabled war veteran (Frost's "Stopping By Woods on a Snowy Evening").

The project is an ongoing archive and an unsystematic (though in its own way ambitious) undertaking, and in no way a statistical survey. But in relation to embarrassment and isolation, uniformity and dissolution, it is interesting that one of the most widely admired poems named by participants, written about by readers of very different ages and levels of sophistication, is "The Love Song of J. Alfred Prufrock," a poem that probes social isolation and social terror with an indelible eloquence. Many high school students seem to intuit that the poem was written by a very young man—Eliot inventing a middle-aged, first-person protagonist as vehicle for the sexual and social diffidence of youth.

Eliot's poem is of course about many other things beside sexual and social fears. For example, it is about culture itself as a burden, as oppressively controlling and crippling as it is enabling—a demanding performance, or at best a diverting performance. Prufrock, that monster of embarrassment, in this sense is very close to the figure of the exhausted aesthete, the wistful dandy. If he had confidence, he might be a dandy: the opposite or reverse of the embarrassed one. For the dandy, experience is somewhat tainted or corrupted by culture. (Though Oscar Wilde might reverse that statement.) As embarrassment is akin to abandonment—feeling excessively distinct from the attentive social world—the aesthete's jadedness is a feeling of sameness. In the terms of Wallace Stevens's "The Man Whose Pharynx Was Bad":

> Mildew of summer and the deepening snow
> Are both alike in the routine I know.

This is partly the voice of the Romantic life of sensation, after it has reached a state of exhaustion. It is an exaggerated, comic version of the premodern poets—Swinburne, Dowson?—who were the immediate predecessors of the Modernist generation. Frost parodies that hypersensitive aesthete in himself, writing in "To Earthward":

> I craved strong sweets, but those
> Seemed strong when I was young.
> The petal of the rose
> It was that stung.

The expressively inverted syntax, "The petal of the rose / it was that stung," is like a gently derisive tone of voice.

What is the point of parodying the dandy or aesthete in oneself, for Eliot or Stevens or Frost? It is, partly, a way of parodying both poetry itself and the democratic culture that offers no ready place for poetry. Like embarrassment (and like the warning "There's someone coming down the road!") the hyperbolic figure of the dandy acknowledges the presence of others and

34

the tension aroused by that presence. I hear this serious joke on the voice of poetry in William Carlos Williams, too. In "These," a poem partly about pathos and death, he writes the terrible then momentarily comical lines:

> the people gone that we loved,
> the beds lying empty, the couches
> damp, the chairs unused—
>
> Hide it away somewhere
> out of the mind, let it get roots
> and grow, unrelated to jealous
>
> ears and eyes—for itself.
> In this mine they come to dig—all.
> Is this the counterfoil to sweetest
>
> music? The source of poetry that
> seeing the clock stopped, says,
> The clock has stopped
>
> that ticked yesterday so well?

Of course all clocks, before they stop, tick—presumably "well." The rhetorical question, repeating the observation, resembles the ancient wisecrack about even a stopped clock being right twice a day. The poem evokes the terror of death and loss, and then for a moment questions elegy and all other attempts to verbalize loss, as tautological or obvious. "Stupidity" has been an element in the poem from the rhetorical snap of its opening sentence:

These

are the desolate, dark weeks
when nature in its barrenness
equals the stupidity of man.

The audacity of this, like the almost-parodic repetition of "the clock has stopped," has a virtuoso quality, in its deadpan, downright way almost as dandified as Stevens's exotic ambushes of vocabulary. There is even a note of the exquisite or dandy in the rarefied word "counterfoil," which sounds like a term from music or fencing but denotes the stub of a check, where the date and amount are recorded.

Like one who recalls "The petal of the rose / It was that stung," and like the sensibility that finds the white of summer mildew and the white of snow "alike," Williams's voice here momentarily concedes an embarrassing absurdity in its discourse, and in the roots of its discourse. The stopped clock once ticked well, then it stopped— poetry sees this and in effect strikes its brow, speaking its question to marvel at the obvious. It is a moment that places poetry into something a little like a roomful of people, with Williams simultaneously among them, regarding poetry as quizzically as any, but also presenting its power to them—as he does with the two lines that follow the relatively comic question:

> The source of poetry that
> seeing the clocked has stopped, says
> The clock has stopped
>
> that ticked yesterday so well?

and hears the sound of lakewater
splashing—that is now stone.

With characteristic speed, restlessly varying idioms and levels, Williams takes the memorializing gesture from somewhat hapless record-keeping—the counterfoil noting the stopped clock—to a somber image, with a kind of classical dignity.

The aesthete, stung by the petal, seeing the mildew and the snow as alike, is in a way the poet reduced to a social type. In these poems, a touch of the hyperbolically exquisite allows poetry to acknowledge its own nature: by some social standards, an art of preposterous, goofball metonymies and far-fetched resemblances. In a mode that is a mirror-reversal of the dandyish, it sees the clock has stopped and says, "The clock has stopped," adding that it ticked quite well yesterday. In each case, a tiny particle of social comedy infuses a brilliant phrase. The self-consciously dandyish and its mock-naive reversal both acknowledge poetry's exorbitant, nearly embarrassing qualities and at the same time make those qualities irresistible and even—because they have a social meaning—somehow familiar.

Poetry, then, has roots in the moment when a voice makes us alert to the presence of another or others. It has affinities with all the ways a solitary voice, actual or virtual, imitates the presence of others. Yet as a form of art it is deeply embedded in the single human voice, in the solitary state that hears the other and sometimes re-creates that other. Poetry is a vocal imagining, ultimately social but essentially individual and inward.

Insofar as Tocqueville was prescient about American poetry's concentration on the human soul, "aloof" from society and from ages, there is perhaps a special drama in our poetry to this play between social and individual, outward and inward voice. Elizabeth Bishop delineates that drama explicitly and compactly in the crucial passage of her poem "In the Waiting Room":

> Suddenly, from inside,
> came an *oh!* of pain
> —Aunt Consuelo's voice—
> not very loud or long.
> I wasn't at all surprised;
> even then I knew she was
> a foolish, timid woman.
> I might have been embarrassed,
> but wasn't. What took me
> completely by surprise
> was that it was *me*:
> my voice, in my mouth.
> Without thinking at all
> I was my foolish aunt,
> I—we—were falling, falling,
> our eyes glued to the cover
> of the *National Geographic*,
> February, 1918.

The voice comes "from inside"—inside the dentist's office and inside the child. The possible embarrassment ("I might have been ... / but wasn't") may be prevented by the strangeness of this moment, which could be a primal moment for poetry, or for individual consciousness, or both. As she begins to faint, the child gazes at the undifferentiated landscape of "shadowy gray knees, / trousers and skirts and boots / and different pairs of hands" and asks "Why should I be my aunt, / or me, or anyone? / What similarities. ... / held us all together / or made us all just one?" The bizarre, alien assemblage of knees and boots, trousers and skirts presents a vision of the social world outside the self, fragmentary and dizzily provisional. The *National Geographic*, that homey compendium of exotic cultures, can offer nothing stranger—or more enigmatically, repellently intimate—than these familiar garments and body parts, in the cultural practices of neck-binding or cannibalism.

What makes us all one—and what makes us

all different—seems deeply involved with a
voice: a voice that is both imagined and actual;
both inner and social; both mine and someone
else's; that separates me and includes me. It will
not do to sentimentalize this voice; at the climax
of Bishop's poem is the sentence "The War was
on." Each of these dualities involves struggle,
perhaps even combat. But the voice of poetry is
uniquely situated as audible yet not necessarily
performative.

The voice of poetry, as in "In the Waiting
Room," is intimate, on an individual scale, but
far from solipsistic. It penetrates and in a sense
originates where the reader's mind reaches toward something heard or uttered as though vocality were one of the senses. This medium is
different from performance: different from the
poet's intonations and personality shining forth
at a poetry reading, and different from a skilled
actor's gifts. The voice is inside a reader, but
gestures outward. Though in many ways it re-

sembles the performer's art, it is in other ways the opposite of that art, for the voice of poetry, though it may be social—and of course has been gloriously theatrical—ultimately begins as profoundly interior. The theatrical art of performance, manifestly and immediately social, moves inward from without, penetrating toward the interior from the spectacularly audible, visible presence. Poetry proceeds in the opposite direction.

IV
Performance

This intimacy and human scale of poetry have special meaning within a mass culture extraordinarily rich in performance—a society where show business and performing arts provide a major industry, a de facto aristocracy, and an all-but-universal measure of things. The mass culture of our democracy, our standard arena for expressing the anxieties of cult and *colon*, is a mighty achievement. And its works have included poetry and been included in poetry. But poetry also plays a significant role as a contrast to mass culture—somewhat resistant precisely because the poetic medium is essentially individual.

This contrast explains the frequency with which poets are asked a certain question. In its various forms, it is the question that the news media cannot easily resist asking any poet. This inevitable inquiry, however it is presented, amounts to: shouldn't poetry be part of show business? Or even, why does poetry seem out of step with the entertainment industry?

And because the query is wrongheaded, asks why poetry is not something other than itself, one's answers are feeble. The form of the question might be, "Have your poems been set to music?" Well yes, but to paraphrase a great poet, I thought I was doing that when I wrote them.

Or, "What about the look of the poem on the page, as visual art?" Fine, attend to it—but as a division of graphics poetry is rather arcane and precious; as an art it is central and major. Or, "What do you think of rap music?" Don't know much about it, but my guess is that as with "literary" poetry, most of it is ordinary, a little of it is very good and a little is contemptible. I have heard Yusef Komunyakaa express distrust of it insofar as it makes a commodity out of rage. "And poetry slams?" Probably a good thing for poetry, though as part of the entertainment industry poetry will always be cute and small; as an art it is immense and fundamental.

But the interrogation is hopeless, because it begins with the assumption that poetry's tremendous strength, in the democratic context—that is, its human scale, its distinction from show business—is its weakness. Poetry as breath penetrates to where the body recognizes the stirring of meaning. Poetry mediates, on a particular and

45

immensely valuable level, between the inner consciousness of the individual reader and the outer world of other people. To take poetry altogether away from that profound terrain to the culturally prominent, more familiar platform of performance is to tame it, because poetry is vocal, but not necessarily performative. The voice of poetry is profoundly resistant to American culture, yet uniquely inside us, as well.

V
Social Presence

I have said that poetry penetrates to where the body recognizes the stirring of meaning. The English language lacks an auditory parallel to "visualization," but in that nameless action of imagining the audible shapes of meanings a crucial human power dwells.

That power is social as well as psychological. If all art is imitation, what does the art of verse imitate? It imitates the social actions of meaning. (This mimesis is all the more distinct if the poem is difficult or aspires to the "nonreferential.") The cadences of poetry mime the shapes of our sentences, our meaningful grunts of exclamation, interrogation, direction, complaint. A line both is and imitates an utterance. (I borrow this idea from John Thompson's brilliant and seminal book *The Founding of English Meter*.) A poem simultaneously says something and in its sounds imitates the action of saying something.

This dual energy acknowledges meaning as a doubly communal phenomenon: communal in one way insofar as it embodies cultural forms, and in another way insofar as it communicates social meanings. To put it differently, in its interior way the voice of poetry is like speaking, but also like watching oneself speak, from another terrain. The stylized, mimetic component, inter-

47

acting with the discursive component, resembles the kind of cognition athletes call "body-knowledge" or musicians refer to as "getting it under your fingers." The poem brings unconscious, inward knowing together with conscious, outward knowing.

As a practical matter, this means that to memorize a poem, or even to say it aloud, or even to "visualize" it in your imaginary voice, schools us in the shapes of meaning. In the singular temporal rhythms of verse, the shapes of meaning become body-knowledge. I wonder if anyone who has memorized a lot of poetry, or heard a lot of it, can fail to write coherent sentences and paragraphs? Possibly, the difficulty many people have in writing sentences manifests a lack of bodily exercise, breath executing patterns of meaning. We try to correct the condition with drills and abstract instructions. Why and how might a professional soldier like Ulysses S. Grant come to write so well? Could it reflect the fact that nineteenth-century Americans recited a lot of poetry, so that the mimesis of meaning came into the region we designate as in our bones or under our skin? Whether that speculation is right or wrong, the ancient relation between poetry and education, verse and understanding, deserves reconsideration.

But this curricular or pedagogical musing is only tangential to the ways poetry's double-nature, simultaneously internal and social, discourse and mimesis, is related to its place in the culture of a democracy. It is time to say something more about The Favorite Poem Project, which invited Americans to submit the title and author of a poem they admired enough to say aloud for a national audio and video archive, and to write a few sentences about the poem's personal importance or significance.

The project has been described in a well-meaning way as an attempt to "promote" or "advance" poetry in the United States, but in fact

49

the main idea was in a sense more passive, and in my opinion more profound: to reflect some of the social presence of poetry in the lives of Americans—implicitly, in relation to our cultural anxieties.

That presence has been doubted, and beyond question the life of poetry has not always been highly visible in the United States—for complex cultural reasons I'll try to sketch. Some people used to envy, and perhaps sentimentalize, the highly visible Soviet-era poetry readings held in Russian sports stadiums and attended by audiences of many thousands. But those events depended not only upon state manipulation and financing, but upon the exploitation of ancient tastes and attitudes: specifically, the stadium readings joined the power of a bureaucratic dictatorship with the cachet of poetry in a country where an angry driver may shout at another "You have no culture!" This is not an American insult. We must strain our imaginations to con-

e of Dickinson and Whitman have served
our readerly voices, as the polished, elo-
and overt myth making of *Hiawatha* and
Midnight Ride of Paul Revere have not.
rofound, engaging absence is suggested by
terms I have quoted from Tocqueville:
hing conceivable is so petty, so insipid, so
ded with paltry interests—in one word, so
poetic—as the life of a man in the United
es." The eclectic, uneven, improvised life of
try in the country reflects that absence and a
ly characteristic response to it. The Favorite
em Project undertook to register specific ex-
ples of Americans who remembered specific
ems. In practice, the undertaking registers the
istence of an American readership as intricate,
s raw, as original, as many-tongued and as ec-
entric as the achievements of the great Ameri-
an poets. The goal was less a promotion than a
elective, indeed edited, portrait.

ceive of countries where the politicians must at least pretend to love the great national poet, and perhaps memorize a line or two. To put it differently, the art has had little snob value among us.

Relatively speaking, in the United States the high bourgeoisie has not preened itself on curatorship of poetry. Nor do we have a single, unifying folk culture—the alternative to a social class that considers itself to have a curatorial role by heredity. The Italian-American grandmother, the Cuban-American grandmother, the Yankee grandmother, the African-American grandmother will pass on different jokes and recipes and rhymes, insofar as they are in the somewhat rare position to pass on anything. And this hypothesis of distinct ethnic or cultural categories is far more pure than our actual, fluid reality.

In place of the aristocratic idea and the folk idea, we have, characteristically, improvised and patched together a place for art and for the art of poetry, in various ways—journalistic, middle-class–domestic, professionalized, academic, self-conscious. The history of this process is reflected by John Hollander's admirable two-volume anthology of nineteenth-century American verse in the Library of America series. ("Verse" is the term Hollander preferred for the title; the publishers insisted on "Poetry," the more honorific word obscuring the social history. Indeed, this little debate is itself part of that history.) The American invention of Creative Writing as a course of study is one example of that improvisation: a means of curating the art, and extending it socially, in the absence of the social institutions and attitudes of Eastern Europe or Asia or Latin America.

This sketch of cultural difference doesn't mean to deprecate American culture, nor to elevate it chauvinistically. The culture is very far from monadic, and it does not have an established place for poetry. We are not Persians or Bengalis. (Though without doubt significant num-

bers of us are indeed Persian
gali-Americans.) That in th
plural cultures most people
compose poetry as part of a life
in each case reflects a particu
and the life of a particular langu
guage, certain forms of memory,
ing, are settled and available, in a

But the eccentricities of Dickins
man also explore the soul's depende
ory, and its resistance to memory,
strangely improvised instruments.
tions of form and lexicon reflect a cu
imported, inherited and invented ele
gle or coalesce; where the provinces
more clear a relation to any capital than
ent is to the past, where the wrestling of
ship with transformation is palpably str
Underlying that contest, and inspiring
tion, is the possibility of a vacuum, of
memory. Thus, the formal singularities

VI
Readers

One question such a portrait might illuminate is the place of poetry in relation to a tremendously powerful, elaborate, and often brilliant mass culture. In one way or another, every American poet and reader must respond to that amazing constellation of genius and vulgarity, vitality and turpitude, of which the greatest products are jazz and the American feature film. The decidedly non-statistical, unscientific nature of the project had the advantage, as well as the limitation, of disregarding numbers in favor of instances.

One of the participants we eventually filmed, John Doherty, wrote in his initial correspondence the sentence "I guess a ditchdigger who reads Shakespeare is still just a ditchdigger." And

55

in the video segment, we do in fact see him digging a ditch, wearing his hardhat, wielding a spade as part of his work as a construction worker for the Boston Gas Company. After talking briefly about his work, he reads some passages from Whitman's "Song of Myself." "Poetry," Doherty says in his remarks, "was definitely intimidating at first. It just looked like a lot of words that were out of order and out of place, that did not belong together." He adds, "It takes a lot of reading and re-reading to grasp it."

I believe that in many countries, social constraints of one kind or another might suppress or temper this candor, requiring more automatic respect, greater dissimulation, or less discovery. This freedom to judge the art of poetry itself as a consumer, intimidated by the art's difficulty but not by its social prestige or authority, feels American to me, for good or ill. It is echoed by a number of the participants, including Seph Rodney, who early in his memorable discussion of Sylvia Plath's "Nick and the Candlestick" remarks that he had always thought of poetry as merely "grandiose" and "for want of a better term, a highfalutin ... not very *real* way of using language." Like Doherty on Whitman, Rodney on Plath presents his attachment to her work as a kind of conversion experience to poetry itself.

Poetry's place in the world and in a particular life seems more self-evident and authoritative for some of the participants who came here from other places, such as Lyn Aye, the Burmese-American anesthesiologist in San Jose, who reads a poem by Zawgee in Burmese and in English translation, or Jayashree Chatterjee, the New Jersey librarian who reads Tagore in Bengali and in English.

What is striking in all four of these instances is a note of personal conviction in both the vocal delivery of the poem each reader selected and in their statements about the poems. The slightly accented Burmese and Indian voices both speak about exile or loss of place, and in what I consider another characteristic American gesture they select poems that simultaneously sharpen and soothe those feelings of homesickness or immigrant dislocation.

In short, the intimacy and introspection of these readers, in their approach to the poems they read, correspond to Tocqueville's proposition about poetry in a democracy. The subject of each poem as they describe it begins with the condition of a soul: material, to borrow Tocqueville's terms, more "vast" for each reader than it is various or "numerous."

Concentration on the individual human soul is audible in the construction worker Doherty's remarkable reading of the closing passage from "Leaves of Grass." The poem's familiar, bizarre mixture of grandiloquence and comedy, egotism and generosity, takes on new overtones as the young man in the video, sitting on an earth-mover, reads the first-person lines:

The spotted hawk swoops by and accuses me . . . he
     complains of my gab and my loitering.

I too am not a bit tamed. . . . I too am
     untranslatable,
I sound my barbaric yawp over the roofs of the
     world.

The last scud of day holds back for me,
It flings my likeness after the rest and true as any on
     the shadowed wilds.
It coaxes me to the vapor and the dusk.

I depart as air. . . . I shake my white locks at the
     runaway sun,
I effuse my flesh in eddies and drift it in lacy jags.

Whitman's vision of his death and his endurance
are read by Doherty as an address to the reader,

on a quite pragmatic level. "You will hardly know who I am or what I mean," he reads, and "Failing to fetch me at first keep encouraged, / Missing me one place search another, / I stop somewhere waiting for you." This advice was written, and in this instance was read, in a particular spirit of direct address, an immediacy that means to redefine poetry itself, and makes the vocal, readerly occasion transcendent.

The mass, technological medium of video, perhaps paradoxically, thus dramatizes something I have called crucial about the medium of poetry: Whitman's lines—visibly—taking for their medium John Doherty's breath and hearing as he both enacts and imagines the sounds of the words and sentences. The artificial occasion of the video reminds me that when I read a poem, aloud or not, I am aware of it as something to say, or that could be said. The vehicle for that awareness is in my bodily senses—a vehicle, also, for memory as when I chant the phone number or the grocery list, manifesting some evolutionary link between vocal rhythm and re-called information.

The reader is not merely the performer of the poem, but an actual, living medium for the poem. Though viewers may feel that Doherty reads the lines well, it is the embodiment of the poem, not his or any performance, that is essential. The poem takes place in each reader, more fundamentally than on any screen or stage. In relation to mass media, this distinction seems to me crucial: if the medium is, above all, any one reader's voice, or any one reader's ears, then the art is by its nature, inherently, on an individual and personal scale.

In its intimacy and human presence, reading a poem may resemble a live performance, as distinct from a mass-produced image such as a movie (or, indeed, a video of someone reciting a poem). Insofar as its text is fixed, the poem, like a play in this respect, is distinctly less ephemeral than the live performance. Poetry's dual qualities of human scale and permanence are roughly parallel to the dread of homogenizing uniformity on one side and the fragmented, violently solipsistic life of the Cyclopes, who have no mores or community, on the other side. Poetry's voice—its literal, actual voice—takes on a heightened poignancy, and a heightened value, in a culture rich in dazzling performative art that is produced, duplicated and marketed on a mass scale.

Spectacle, too, is not the point. A principle in making the videos was never to illustrate the poem: no footage of a snow man for Wallace Stevens's "The Snow Man." In the setting of mass culture, the voice of poetry, in ways that entertainment media cannot, embodies something crucially different from spectacle: an intense concentration on individual consciousness.

To put this another way, the videos reveal that one can see a person read a poem. I can watch your face while you listen to music, watch a movie, or look at visual art—but I am not wit-nessing your experience of that work. The same goes for watching a reader deep in a novel. To watch someone saying a poem aloud can be to witness that person's experience of the poem. The readers in the videos, though they know that they are being filmed, make visible the inti-mate and singular penetration of the art. Their "performances" of the poems are not artistic performances. The reader's voice is different from actorly interpretations of the poem's emo-tions and ideas—though those are surely pres-ent—but something subtly different from that: presentations of what it is like when Seph Rodney or Lynn Aye or John Doherty reads a particular poem.

Tocqueville's speculations about equality on one hand, and on the other contemporary mass culture with its emphasis on performance, on lavish spectacle and reproduction, combine to make me hear with special urgency the particular reader's voice: its regional accent, its sense of an individual life, and its relation to the cadences and meanings of the words, as it utters:

> You will hardly know who I am or what I mean,
> But I shall be good health to you nevertheless,
> And filter and fiber your blood.

VII
The Narcissistic and the Personal

When the Favorite Poem Project has been described approvingly as "populist" I have felt uncomfortable, because I know that the approach was in essential ways elitist. There is a generation that loves the writing of Robert Service, and some of them wrote cogent letters in response to the project, and some of their grandchildren wrote about Shel Silverstein. Some from the generations between those two wrote to us about

Rod McKuen, or the lyrics of Bob Dylan—all part of the larger archive of letters and e-mails, and significant elements in that archive, but not represented in the book or the recordings, by fiat of us editors.

On the other hand, we were guided by respect for the ways nonprofessional readers read and the ways they describe their reading. This element of the project has excited some negative judgment. Pov Chin, a teenager from California who is represented both in the anthology and in the videos, wrote:

> My interpretation of this poem written by Langston Hughes may not be the same as his. But a poem is what I choose to make of it and this one is a description of me. It explains how I feel about life.

A reviewer took this statement as his leading example of a defect he found in the book. After quoting these sentences, he writes:

This theme—*this is a description of me*—occurs again and again. . . . Rather than letting poems draw us out of ourselves, making us larger and broader, we are encouraged to make the poems smaller so that we can take them inside us and, in a literal sense, comprehend them. . . . Pinsky and Dietz may simply have assumed that the only way to sell poetry to Americans is to appeal to their inherent narcissism.*

In its way, this makes a certain sense. (The reviewer, incidentally, quotes Tocqueville about American pettiness and self-centeredness, but not about the "more vast" subjects for poetry.) The terms of the Favorite Poem invitation did invite the volunteers to say something about their particular, personal reasons for selecting the poem. Indeed, when putting together the anthology and the recordings, an explicit criterion for selection was the intensity and interest

*Troy Jollimore, *Boston Book Review*, March 2000.

of what the reader had to say about the poem. It could be argued that this editorial inclination vulgarized the project, or at least distorted it toward the personal or introspective, and away from the poem as a means of discovery about the world, or as a highly developed work of art.

But the cliche of American narcissism does not adequately describe what these people actually say. Let me return to the example of Pov Chin, who says, "this poem is a description of me." Her voice and accent in the video are those of a California teenager, and this prefatory statement of hers (partly a statement, in my understanding of it, of diffidence) can sound glib or self-centered. The poem is an extremely short one by Langston Hughes, far from his most impressive work:

Minstrel Man

Because my mouth
Is wide with laughter

And my throat
Is deep with song,
You do not think
I suffer after
I have held my pain
So long?
Because my mouth
Is wide with laughter,
You do not hear
My inner cry?
Because my feet
Are gay with dancing,
You do not know
I die?

The little paradigm of this poem, as plain as a folk song, takes on rich overtones and vibrations in relation to the American minstrel tradition of blackface—makeup that was sometimes worn by black, as well as white, performers. The grinning minstrel-show performer, bursting with joy, represents a terrible and complicated process of cultural appropriation and distortion, all sorts of sublimated guilts and envies and myths, comforting and disturbing.

Of all that, the young student Pov Chin appears to have been unaware. When she found the poem and copied it out, she tells us, she had not heard of Langston Hughes. It is not clear if she knew at the time that he was African-American, or what the information signifies to her, particularly since she was born in Laos of Cambodian parents. Yet what she says about the poem is historically germane, and perhaps increases one's esteem for Hughes's poem. In the book, she writes:

I am not free. I am a female Cambodian growing up in America but I am raised in the old-fashioned Cambodian ways. Asian tradition for daughters is very strict. It is so hard for me to see my friends having a sleep-over and the only person missing is me. I walk around school with a big smile on my face but inside I am a caged bird just waiting to be free. Life has never been easy for me especially with my parents' problems. Their problems started during the Khmer Rouge genocide in the early '70s. Two of their sons passed away in front of their faces, killed by the Khmer Rouge. They still had the courage to get out of Cambodia and find refuge for us in America.

This is not literary criticism, nor does it pretend to be. But the word for it is not "narcissism," either, and as an explanation of why the writer values "Minstrel Man" by Langston Hughes, it is forceful and appropriate. The association of freedom and cultural restraint with performance, the equation of "big smile" with being caged, represent an insightful tribute to Hughes's poem. To the extent that Pov Chin didn't know much about the author, it is remarkably intuitive. Even the exclusion from the American

70

high-school custom of sleep-overs and the delicate euphemism "passed away" for the murdered children testify to a rich and respectful relation to the poem.

The distinction between the narcissistic and the personal, abundantly clear in this letter quoted in the anthology, is even more clear in the video segment artfully filmed by Emiko Omori. In the opening shot Pov Chin begins speaking in the foreground; in the background, behind her, we see a suburban-looking interior and first a television set playing something with Asian faces and language and then, as the camera pans upward, the seated figure of a woman. This watchful figure, present throughout the shot, is clearly Pov Chin's mother, silently following the interview as though she is not willing to let this, one of her remaining children, out of her sight. We see a shrine, and some incense being lit and some family photographs: of children posing in front of a modest house; of an unsmiling elderly woman.

A notable aspect of Pov Chin's narration comes

with her explanation that during the family ordeal and the murder of the little boys she was
not yet born; the mother was pregnant. "It was
not only us," she says, "it was my granny, too,
and they killed my granny." The first person
plural of "only us" is striking: "they rounded us
up" she says at another point. This unselfconscious first-person plural, like the watching
maternal figure, embodies the powerful familial
and social component of the sentences quoted in
the anthology, and echoes similar questions of
the generic and the individual, inside and outside, cultural cage and cultural sustenance, in
Hughes's poem. The first-person singular of "I
am not free" is related to the first-person plural
of "they rounded us up"; both sentences acknowledge the great conundrum of each person's connection to others. Whatever one understands that "we" to represent, it is not
narcissism.

I have quoted a somewhat negative response

to the project (and the review I've quoted from is in fact only partly negative) less to contradict it than to suggest the range of cultural and literary responses that this undertaking has called up, partly by accident. Questions about an anthology, or about what is narcissistic, what is personal, are ripples in a great flood of ambiguities and agitations. My proposition is that the reviewer's gesture against a leveling uniformity and the Favorite Poem Project's gesture toward a unifying cultural ground, though they seem like opposite actions, both express a somewhat anxious defense—or pursuit—of shared memory.

VIII
Models of Culture

A successful, inventive mass culture, together with Tocqueville's "principle of equality" from which the mass culture partly grows, have engendered a need to define, and perhaps to construct, the social place of an ancient art. This pressure should not be seen as merely negative; it, too, is enabling as well as controlling. The mass culture itself struggles to adjust memory and change, and like the poets it sometimes succeeds and sometimes collapses into pretension or banality. In the absence of the settled aristocratic idea, and in the absence of the unifying folk culture, Americans have been pressed to supply new forms of memory.

Responding to this pressure, Whitman became brokenhearted by his inability to create (and fill) the role of national bard. That sadness was re-enforced for me by my own rather naive surprise at how journalists responded to President Clinton's gift of *Leaves of Grass* to Monica Lewinsky: they apparently thought of Whitman not as the quintessential American poet, but as the author of a rather hot book.

Nonetheless, the vacuum or pressure that created and frustrated Whitman's ambitions also inspired his mighty and mightily driven achievement. And the unsettled place of poetry has continued to inspire great works as well as blather and despair: the poetry of both William Carlos Williams and Wallace Stevens, for example, can be seen as growing more or less explicitly out of the question of poetry's place in national manners. "The spirit and space," writes Stevens in his poem "The American Sublime": "The empty spirit / In vacant space. / What wine does one drink? / What bread does one eat?" To take a less sublime example, improvising the figurative bread, the wine, the place, Americans have invented MFA degrees, poetry slams, coffee houses, small press cooperatives: sometimes gawky, yet sometimes vital or excellent cultural structures. The audio recordings, videos and anthology of the Favorite Poem Project are one more gesture of this kind of improvisation, and in some measure give an account of that improvisation, as well.

I'm afraid that to make my point I may have exaggerated the uniqueness of the United States. All culture, after all, like any living person's memory, perpetually adds and rearranges, drops and inflects its material: culture is a process of change and adaptation, not a static entity or a list of works. The more I knew about Iran and India, the more, I am sure, I would have to modify my assumptions about Persian and Bengali poetry, and their readership as I imagine it, talking through my hat—the more flux and ambiguity I would perceive.

Still, American culture as I have experienced it seems so much in process, so brilliantly and sometimes brutally in motion, that standard models for it fail to apply. The Mandarin notion of a privileged elite preserving cultural goods on an old-world model is swamped by the demotic genius of characteristic makers like Herman

Melville, Emily Dickinson, Preston Sturges, Duke Ellington, William Carlos Williams. The Arnoldian model of cultural missionaries' bringing along the masses wilts not only for the same reason but because modern political history has discredited the notion that intellectual or artistic figures can, automatically or by their nature, serve as moral leaders. The Mandarin's complementary opposite, the Philistine model, would accept the marketplace entirely: whatever is consumed is good. This idea collapses before the omnivorous, strangely vaunting aspiration of actual Americans—with the Favorite Poem Project one current source of examples. Another model, the idea of mass culture as our only real culture, cannot do because culture is a process of memory, and as mass cultural products speed by, the popular culture of each decade is winnowed to be preserved in the care of universities, libraries, foundations. A serious task of criticism is to assist in that winnowing process. In the archives of curatorship, classic jazz and silent comedy and blues await any of the best of our sitcoms or rap performers that deserve remembering.

And the model of American culture as a mere confederation of ethnic or regional or religious or gender-based cultures cannot suffice. Our greatest achievements—a poem by Dickinson or a chorus by Parker—are as mixed, syncretic and eclectic as our inventions in food or clothing. In that polyglot, heuristic and erratic flux, each of the non-professional readers included in the recordings, anchored by the vocal attachment to a poem, offers a reference point: the impurity and idiosyncracy of a cultural fact.

The culture has no model as a fixed state or a curriculum: it is a process, characterized by unanticipated shifts and improvisations. Nor is it necessary to sentimentalize that process. Triviality and pedantry, bigotry and complacency—these aspects of the larger culture, too, could be reflected by the microcosm of the letters received by the Favorite Poem Project, if that were its goal. Poetry is not the voice of virtue and right thinking—not the rhyme department of any progressive movement. It is a commonplace that great poets have espoused repulsive politics. The turns of verse, between justified and ragged, the regular and the unique, the spoken and the implied, the private and the social, profoundly embody not a moral, but a cultural quest for life between a barren isolation on one side and an enveloping mass on the other. That quest is the action of poetry's voice.

IX
Conclusion

I will quote one of my own favorite poems—one I have written about before, in an account of my home town on the Jersey Shore. Written near the beginning of the twentieth century by

Edwin Arlington Robinson, "Eros Turannos" epitomizes for me the tidal forces within lyric poetry that draw it toward social reality. The poem's peculiar, rather spectacular form embodies those forces and their "War," as Bishop calls it, with something private and interior. In its title and other echoes of Greek tragedy, in its focus on one heroic figure in her choral, provincial setting, "Eros Turannos" recalls the individual's cultural anxieties of suffocation on one side and an isolating dearth on the other.

The protagonist is a woman who must choose between a love affair that she well knows will be a calamity, or no love affair at all. The extraordinary account of her psychology turns out, partway through the poem, to be voiced by a town, in the first person plural:

Eros Turannos

She fears him, and will always ask
What fated her to choose him;

80

She meets in his engaging mask
    All reasons to refuse him;
But what she meets and what she fears
Are less than are the downward years
Drawn slowly to the foamless weirs
    Of age, were she to lose him.

Between a blurred sagacity
    That once had power to sound him,
And Love, that will not let him be
    The Judas that she found him,
Her pride assuages her almost,
As if it were alone the cost.
He sees that he will not be lost,
    And waits and looks around him.

A sense of ocean and old trees
    Envelops and allures him;
Tradition, touching all he sees,
    Beguiles and reassures him;
And all her doubts of what he says
Are dimmed with what she knows of days—

Till even prejudice delays,
    And fades, and she secures him.

The falling leaf inaugurates
    The reign of her confusion;
The pounding wave reverberates
    The dirge of her illusion;
And home, where passion lived and died,
Becomes a place where she can hide,
While all the town and harbor side
    Vibrate with her seclusion.

We tell you, tapping on our brows,
    The story as it should be,
As if the story of a house
    Were told, or ever could be;
We'll have no kindly veil between
Her visions and those we have seen,
As if we guessed what hers have been,
    Or what they are or would be.

Meanwhile we do no harm; for they
    That with a god have striven,

Not hearing much of what we say,
　　Take what the god has given;
Though like waves breaking it may be,
Or like a changed familiar tree,
Or like a stairway to the sea
　　Where down the blind are driven.

The astoundingly deployed rhymes make "Eros Turannos" a kind of hyper-ballad: a ballad to the ballad power, as though the woman's isolation and shame call up some longing for a folk-tradition that her surroundings cannot provide. On this level, Thompson's idea that the cadences of verse imitate the shape of sentences has a kind of palpable application. More explicitly, the first-person plural as "we" tap our brows and tell the story impersonates the communal, but also heightens the central character's loneliness and lack.

That lack is made more poignant for me by what I know of Robinson's career. For the long first part of it, he was indigent, lonely, spurned by magazine editors, embittered with his provincial town in Maine and with the New York where he also found the going hard.

But on the other hand, the town does notice the woman's fate, and registers it and recounts it with awe. On this subject, let me quote the letter about this poem quoted in *Americans' Favorite Poems*—the only letter in the anthology that we editors print anonymously:

I discovered the poem many years ago as a newly married girl living in a small town, which in fact possesses a harborside. My husband had an intractable (it seemed then) drug and alcohol problem and was away a lot for his job. I didn't have a job at the time, knew no one, and spent many days in solitude riding my bike, reading, and reflecting on what my life had become since my decision to marry. I did not then comprehend what the line "for they that with a god have striven" meant. I just recognized completely the state of wishing to be united with a man because of what I knew or thought I knew about the onward years. I lived then and now in an ancient house left me by my father, whose father left it to him, whose father left it to him. It is one mile from the ocean, surrounded by old trees. These facts made up no small part of my husband's decision to marry me. I copied that poem into the journal I kept then and it sits before me on the table as I write. I have always felt the woman was as I was. The knowledge that I've gained about "the god" has lent a retrospective dignity to events experienced as utter failure. The discovery of the poem, with its eerily large number of coincidences with my own situation, was like a gift, or maybe a clue in a giant game of charades, from "the god" himself, who saw he had perhaps misjudged his opponent.

This personal account of the poem is as remarkable as the coincidences it notes. Its viewpoint is perhaps more psychological and social than literary. The writer, for all her power and eloquence, does not choose to consider the ways that the poem's story may be Robinson's story, a transformed account of his own frustration, loneliness, dignity and rage. But this insightful, anonymous letter also suggests something like the classical relation of tragic hero and community, or touches on that idea with the words "a retrospective dignity." In the poem, the community gains a certain stature from its awareness that in it is one who has wrestled with a god; the individual gains dignity from the witnessing of that struggle. The man, who "waits and looks around him," is in a significant way less important than the god or the town. The poem is less about two people than it is about one person, who deals with love as a ruling force, and with a social setting.

The form of poetry in "Eros Turannos," the chiming and symmetrically swirling rhymes, give rich voice to a great solitude, a desolation that communicates itself to the very landscape. "A sense of ocean and old trees" is vague partly as a mocking evocation of the man who looks around him, lightly comic in a way like the "iron clothing" of Robinson's nostalgist Miniver Cheevy. But the phrase also has a specificity that relates it to Robinson's concluding image, the "stairway to the sea / Where down the blind are driven." The nightmare ritual or flight suggested by that image calls up a social world more ancient or more fantastically barbarian than can be known. The voice of the poem, in our heads and in our breath, brings that archaic world and the solitude of the protagonist together, with terror and majesty.

"Eros Turannos" was published in the same issue of *Poetry* magazine as Carl Sandburg's group of *Chicago Poems*, including "Chicago"— the well-known anthology piece (it appears in the Favorite Poem anthology), the prolonged apostrophe that begins "Hog Butcher for the World" and ends "Freight Handler to the Nation." "Chicago" is not a bad piece of writing, despite the limitations I have indicated with the phrase "anthology piece." In no way does it begin to equal "Eros Turannos" in emotion, in formal penetration or invention.

But Sandburg's group was made the leading item in that issue of *Poetry*, and that year received the magazine's Levinson Prize, which Yvor Winters in his book on Robinson says was "the most considerable prize offered for poetry in the United States at that time."* With the arrogance of the living, we may deceive ourselves that nowadays we know better. What's germane here is the way these two poems approach their subjects, and their implied subject of how poetry will situate itself in relation to American life.

It may be that the judges admired the vitality

*Winters, *Edwin Arlington Robinson* (New York: Norton, 1971), p. 11.

of Sandburg's epithets and participles: "Laughing the stormy, husky, brawling laughter of
Youth, half-naked, sweating, proud to be Hog
Butcher. . . . " Indeed, they may have found his
poem engaging and engaged precisely in relation
to my subject in these lectures: poetry's voice in
American culture. Where "Eros Turannos" might
have seemed laudable but modest in scope—a
character study or an anecdote—Sandburg's di-
thyrambic embrace of Chicago as "laughing with
white teeth" may have seemed not only original
but *avant-garde*.

Comparison of the two poems helps define a
place for American poetry, its profound role of
both engaging and resisting the rather Sand-
burgesque giant of a society that is at once dazzling and banal, provincial and global, menacing
and hopeful. Poetry's voice participates in that
society and its culture, but by its nature also resists them: singular where they are plural, mem-
ory-driven where they are heedless, personal

where they are impersonal—luxuriously slow where they are rushed, and thrillingly swift where they are plodding.

I speak as an enthusiast of modern life: I enjoy the possibilities of jet travel, the DVD and the VCR, am devoted to my computer and my cell phone, appreciate the marvels of contemporary plumbing, medicine, dentistry. Like Frank Bidart in his recent poem "For the Twentieth Century," I am grateful for the technologies that make Callas, Laurel & Hardy, Szigeti available at a touch of the PLAY button, turning their art into "pattern, form / whose infinite // repeatability within matter / defies matter." But the voice that appreciates the artists and the "thousand / technologies of ecstasy" that preserve them is also idiosyncratic, not duplicable, and resistantly inward as well as outward.

What Robinson resisted in 1911 was a provincial vacuum, the nightmare of us small-town watchers who can gossip and tap our brows but cannot make tragedies or ballads. A village stinginess haunts his work and this poem in particular, recalling Tocqueville's description of American life: "so petty, so insipid, so crowded with paltry interests." There is something heroic in Robinson's simultaneous resistant loathing and meticulous love for the provincial settings and figures he imagined, the lonely grandeur of his hypertrophied ballad stanzas and saturated ironies. Devising a courtly telling for the materials of barren gossip, Robinson suggests the rich enigmas and promises of the American setting. Sandburg has considerable merits, but by comparison his poem's rebellions are trivial, and its celebrations coarse.

"Chicago" responds to the dread of sectarian dissolution, of a culture too weak to hold together, by constructing a brilliant but rather bullying journalistic rhetoric that is covertly general, for all its apparent specificity: there is no specter of isolation in his poem because he does not include even the possibility of loneliness. In another direction, "Chicago" deals with anxiety about an enveloping, centralized mass culture with expert, infectious pep-talk: what Sandburg's poem resists, ultimately, is discouragement. As an ostensible "barbaric yawp" it is studied and domesticated.

Robinson, like the hero of his poem, wrestled with something larger than himself, and like hers his wrestling deserves a grave and enthralled communal awe. His peculiar blend of ballad and tragedy, meditation and gossip, resists the cultural stereotypes and the literary clichés of his own time and of ours. His command of specificity and abstraction, his managing of idiom and lines, resist in an anticipatory way any invitation to make American poetry something that goes down easily: a part of show business, or a branch of literary theory, or any other diminished thing.

"Eros Turannos" is arresting and spectacular,

in the chamber of spirit and ear that I have suggested is the place of poetry. It answers and evokes our anxieties about mass culture with an individual, enigmatic fate. It answers and evokes our anxieties about fragmentation with the fiery ingenuity of its cadences, the audacity of its references. To the American thesis of a deadening absence of culture and its antithesis, a devouring omniculture, the poem responds with a synthesis that includes both a provincial tapping of our brows and the image of the blind driven down a stairway to the sea—all in the single breath of the poet's invention. Robinson's homely word "house" makes the fate-driven family of Atreus simultaneous with the pilasters and spandrels of a seaside village manse.

These are the inclusions and audacities of American art: not tamed by expectation, untranslatable by journalism or pedantry, outlandish, even barbaric, sounding its yawps somewhere over our worldly roofs, or beyond them.

Index